The CUSTOMER is always WRONG

The CUSTOMER is alWays WRONG

Funny Stories and Tales of Horror From My Life In the Food Service Industry

Adam Ballarino

authorHOUSE®

AuthorHouse™
1663 Liberty Drive
Bloomington, IN 47403
www.authorhouse.com
Phone: 1-800-839-8640

© 2012 by Adam Ballarino. All rights reserved.

No part of this book may be reproduced, stored in a retrieval system, or transmitted by any means without the written permission of the author.

Published by AuthorHouse   10/23/2012

ISBN: 978-1-4772-7761-4 (sc)
ISBN: 978-1-4772-7760-7 (hc)
ISBN: 978-1-4772-7762-1 (e)

Library of Congress Control Number: 2012919275

Any people depicted in stock imagery provided by Thinkstock are models, and such images are being used for illustrative purposes only.
Certain stock imagery © Thinkstock.

Because of the dynamic nature of the Internet, any web addresses or links contained in this book may have changed since publication and may no longer be valid. The views expressed in this work are solely those of the author and do not necessarily reflect the views of the publisher, and the publisher hereby disclaims any responsibility for them.

For Jennifer

My sister Jennifer worked in the food service industry for close to twenty years. Jenbal, as her friends called her, saw and heard more ridiculous things from customers than anybody could ever imagine. If I used any of her experiences in this book it would be thicker than "War and Peace". Although these are all my own stories, my conversations with Jennifer were a driving force in me documenting them all.

I started writing all this to deal with my anger towards all the ignorant people I dealt with everyday. A couple months after I started I ran into the proverbial wall and just couldn't finish a thought without getting frustrated and frazzled. Then, one day a tragic thing happened.

Jennifer lost her long battle with cancer. I promised myself this book was going to be completed as a tribute to my sister and friend Jenbal.

This book is completed because of Jennifer. This book is mine to have forever because of Jennifer. This book is here for you to enjoy because of Jennifer. She will forever be in my heart and hopefully yours also. Jen I miss you and I love you.

"Unfortunately, common sense is not all that common".
-Eric Cusson, Close friend

Contents

Preface	The Customer is Always Wrong...	xi
Introduction	Let's Get This Out of the Way Now..............................	xv
Chapter 1	What the Hell is a "Cinema Pub"?.....................................	1
Chapter 2	The First Story..	5
	Quickie # 1 Everybody Enjoys a Quickie......................	9
Chapter 3	Bad Boys, Bad Boys, Whatcha Gonna Do	11
	Quickie # 2...	15
Chapter 4	I'm an Asshole	17
	Quickie #3..	21
Chapter 5	Bruschetta Biiiiiiiiiitch..	23
	Quickie #4..	29
Chapter 6	Racist Bastards	31
	Quickie #5..	35
Chapter 7	Sorry, I Don't Know the Score......................................	37
	Quickie #6..	43
Chapter 8	Wrong Cinema Pub Asshole..	45
	Quickie #7..	49
Chapter 9	Urination Deja Vu..	51
	Quickie #8..	55
Chapter 10	Thanks for Your Concern Officer..................................	57
	Quickie #9..	61
Chapter 11	Butch Lesbians...	63
	Quickie #10..	67
Chapter 12	Rubber Gun..	69
	Quickie #11..	73
Chapter 13	Daughter's Birthday...	75
	Quickie #12..	81
Chapter 14	Do I Have a What?...	83
	Quickie #13..	87
Chapter 15	What the Fuck Happened to You?.................................	89
About the Author...		97

Preface

The Customer is Always Wrong

I spent ten years working as a manager in the food service industry. They were the most miserable ten years of my life. Every day I would think to myself that today would have to be better than the last. There is no way it could get any worse. Yet, every day I was proven wrong.

Just when I thought that I had dealt with the most ignorant person on the planet, the actual holder of "The Most Ignorant Person on the Planet" heavyweight belt would walk through the door.

Considering I have what some people would classify as a bad temper it is a miracle that I lasted that long without going "Postal" (My apologies to all the fine men and women working for The United Postal Service. But if the shoe fits, wear it).

The main reason I made it that long is that I found by coming home and writing about the absolutely ridiculous, ignorant, stupid, absurd, misinformed, inbred, mental midgets, (insert your favorite adjective here), helped me deflect a lot of the bitter anger and disgust that I would build up on a nightly basis.

The ages old saying of "The Customer Is Always Right" is the biggest bunch of bullshit that I have ever heard. It has about as much truth to it as when Monica said "No Mr. President, of course I won't keep the dress. By the way these are great cigars, thank you".

If you ask anyone who has ever worked in the industry they will either agree with me or they are a liar. The simple fact of the matter is that based on the extensive scientific studies I have conducted on this social epidemic (No public funds were used for this research. I applied for a grant but was told the money was earmarked for the old "Butter vs. Margarine" debate) the customer is wrong nine out of ten times.

The majority of the time it is just some miserable son of a bitch that just wants everybody else to be just as miserable as they are. "Misery Loves Company" is the motto they live by and they plan on having as much company as they can. Other times it is just a person (word being used loosely) that feels that the fact they are spending money means they own the person they are handing that money to.

Whatever the back story with these assholes is, nothing makes it right. If you're an unhappy piece of shit keep it to yourself. Don't take it out on somebody that's trying to make a living but is unfortunate enough to be the first person you see after you receive the letter informing you that after twenty years on welfare it is time to get a job.

As you may have noticed in the first few paragraphs, I am not a professional writer. You may also have noticed that on certain topics I am opinionated. You would be correct in your observations. My opinions, however, are not the reason I wrote this book.

I wrote this book out of self preservation. I wrote it to keep me from coming home at night and screaming at my beautiful wife about something a fucking asshole that is one notch above Phreatobius Cistemarum on the evolutionary chart had done that night to piss me off. I wrote it to keep me from driving off the highway at a high rate of speed just to end the misery.

Every word you are hopefully about to read is true. This shit actually happened. If I had the imagination to make this stuff up, Stephen King and I would be neighbors in a small town in Maine and my horror stories would be scaring the shit out of the master himself.

I am not stupid enough to think that what I write here will make all these idiots change their ways. Most of them probably can't even read. (Thank God for books on tape) Maybe, just maybe, one of them will see this and realize how stupid they have acted and then share their enlightenment at the next "Assholes of the World Unite" meeting. It can only make this world a better place.

In all fairness to my customers they were not the only ones who made my life as miserable as a gerbil just purchased by Richard Gere on a weekend bender. (Insert your own joke here. Yes I said insert.) My employees also drove me to the point where I had Jack Kervorkian on speed dial.

Although they drove me crazier than Mike Tyson with a Rubiks Cube, I have changed their names to protect the stupid. Without the ineptness of these fine men and women I would not have as much to bitch about. So that is what I am going to do. BITCH. Hopefully you stick around for more. If not, just remember to try the veal and make sure to tip your waitress.

Introduction

Let's Get This Out of the Way Now

After I had written a decent sample size of this pure stupidity I gave it to a friend of mine to look over and give me his opinions and feedback. This was a friend whose opinions I really did and still do respect. Before I gave it to him though, I explained to him that it was simply a really rough first draft. I told him that most of what he was going to read had been written while I was still extremely pissed off because this shit had just happened to me and my anger was unfiltered at the time. I told him that there would be grammatical mistakes. I told him I didn't care about run on sentences at that point (I still don't give a shit about run on sentences for that matter). I explained that I was trying to relate to people like myself—normal, everyday, hardworking people. I told him that it was the true meaning of reality and that if I happened to write motherfucker three times in one sentence it was because I had really said motherfucker three times in one sentence.

    He obviously listened to me about as much as my wife does. About as much as Pee Wee Herman listened when his mother told him public masturbation would cause blindness.

    When my friend returned the pages to me they looked like a midterm on socialism that the professor was returning to the student who only got into college so the school could reach a quota that would kick in a federal grant. There was more red ink than the federal budget (I'm thinking eliminate all those aforementioned grants). The problem though, wasn't just that he corrected the spelling, the grammar, or the way my paragraphs began and ended. The problem was all the notes he wrote on the side of the pages. The fucking thing looked like the first draft of a Beethoven symphony.

My reason for starting to write all this bullshit down was to simply get it off my chest without exploding in anger. It was to keep me from inflicting serious bodily harm on some fucking moron that had just pissed me off without even realizing they were the one at fault and I was just trying to do my job. Instead of going ballistic on some dickhead who insisted in getting his money back because "Gigli" didn't live up to his expectations (dickhead really isn't a strong enough way to describe anybody that had high expectations for "Gigli"). I would instead write it all down and then try to forget about it for the moment.

My problem is that I would like nothing better than to stop after work for a few beers with my friends and unload all the days frustrations on them. It's tit for tat. You tell me your tales of woe and I will tell you mine. It's the principal reason local bars can stay in business. If none of your friends are there than you bitch to the bartender. Unfortunately for me, all my friends have normal 9 to 5 jobs. I, on the other hand don't usually get out of work until midnight or later. So unfortunately, other than my wife there is no one to bitch to. This is the reason the laptop became my best friend (the unlimited porn availability didn't hurt either). The best part of this friendship (besides the porn) is that I don't have to listen to the laptops problems. I eliminate all the bullshit work talk I have to listen to while I wait for my turn to rant. BRILLIANT.

My point of all this babble is that I didn't write this to please all you "Scholars of the English Language." I wrote it for every bartender, waitress, waiter, host, hostess, cook, barback, busboy, delivery driver, and most of all, manager that ever had to just suck it up and kiss the ass of some complete fucking asshole because society deems that's the way it's supposed to be.

Most of all I wrote it for me and I wrote it the way I talk. The way I would tell a story to a friend other than my laptop. A friend I could sit and have a beer with. My life is NC-17 and I'm not going to change. I call a spade a spade. Hell, sometimes I even call it a fucking shovel.

Chapter 1

What the Hell is a "Cinema Pub"?

In order for you to understand the stories that you are hopefully going to be reading shortly, I first need to explain what a "Cinema Pub" is. Despite what all my past customers think, it is not a difficult concept to grasp. All you have to do is break the name down.

The following is from "The World English Dictionary"

Cinema (`sinima)

—n

1. Chiefly (Brit) a. a place designed for the exhibition of films b. (as modified): a cinema seat

2. the cinema a. the art or business of making films b. films collectively

Pub (p^b)

—n

1. Chiefly (Brit) formal name: public house a building with a bar and one or more public rooms licensed for the sale and consumption of alcoholic drink, often also providing light meals

2. (Austral), (NZ) a hotel

Put the two together and you get a place where you can watch first run movies while you have a meal and some libations all at the same time. It is dinner and a movie all rolled into one. For most people this idea was as foreign and unimaginable as Marion Barry getting elected again as the Mayor of D.C.(That one still disturbs me. I guess a little crack, some hookers, and a videotape never hurt anybody).

My political views aside, I don't understand why some people could not fathom having a steak and a beer at the same time as they are watching Denzel Washington stuff an explosive device up the ass of the man responsible for Dakota Fanning being kidnapped (probably not the best reference I could have used but it is a great movie).

Seriously though, all we did was eliminate one of the two decisions you would normally have to make on date night. Instead of having to decide on which restaurant you would go to first and then which movie you would see, all you have to do now is choose the movie. We had the consumer in mind from the beginning.

It's simple really. You walk in and tell the nice person behind the ticket counter which film you would like to watch. Then you are shown which theater that movie is playing in. When you go into the theater it is set up like a restaurant except for the movie screen at the front of the theater and all the speakers along the walls. A waiter or waitress takes your order for food and drinks while you wait for the start of the movie. Then, hopefully just as the lights dim and the movie begins, the food is brought to your table, and you enjoy.

There is always a waiter or waitress in the theater while the movie is playing so if you would like another drink or something else to eat they can take care of it for you. Then, as the credits roll you pay your bill and discuss the movie with your friends as you exit the theater.

See how easy that is to understand. Yet, I have a harder time explaining this concept to the customers than I would be explaining good parenting to Joan Crawford. They just don't get it.

All that aside, I hope you get the idea of what the cinema pub is all about. It will make the rest of this nonsense a lot more enjoyable to read. So let's go, shall we?

Chapter 2

The First Story

The first story took place only a few weeks after the cinema pub opened. At first I thought it was an isolated incident and probably just dumb luck that it happened so soon. I figured that it was probably a good thing to get this out of the way so quickly. I thought that this was clearly going to be the exception and not the rule.

HOLY SHIT was I wrong. As it turned out this was a foreshadowing of what I would have to deal with practically every night for the next ten years of my life. It would be all downhill from here and there was nothing I could do about it. Except there was something I could do about it. Fight back was the approach I took from the beginning and it is the only way I made it as long as I did.

It's nine thirty on a busy Saturday night. Both movies have started, and all the food has gone out. Everything is running smooth (so I think). I go out back to the loading dock to have a cigarette. I'm enjoying my first moment of peace all day when I notice a woman slither through the railing outside the side door. All of a sudden she went straight down face first like Jenna Jamison upon hearing the director yell action.

Now being someone that enjoys an adult beverage myself, I can empathize with somebody who may have had too much. Unfortunately this woman didn't really give me much to work with.

"Are you alright maam?" I ask immediately.

"I'm fucking fine." She so eloquently responded.

After that response to my mild yet good Samaritan like attempt to help this scholar of the English language, I decided that she was on her own. Unfortunately, she had other plans.

As it turned out she had to urinate. The only problem was that she apparently didn't realize there were bathrooms inside (I understand it's a new concept but come on). This fine upstanding member of the community proceeded to walk over to where I was standing and do something that has taken years of therapy for me to erase from my permanent memory bank.

She dropped her pants and underwear and started pissing right there at my feet. There have not been many times in my life when I have been speechless, but this was one of those rare times.

Like a gentleman (because I was completely at a loss for words) I waited until she was done using the facilities (pissing on my shoes) and then asked her the question that I obviously already knew the answer to.

"Did you just piss on my feet ?" I asked completely dumbfounded.

"So fucking what?" Spewed from her "What the fuck are you gonna do about it?"

"I'm going to throw you the fuck out. That's what I'm gonna do." I screamed as I took my shoes off and threw them in the dumpster. "You are leaving NOW."

"No" She cried. "You can't throw us out."

When I heard her say those last words it made me smile for a second. The first reason I smiled was the fact that I have grown to love it when a customer tells me I can't do something. More importantly though, was that she used the word US. That meant there was at least one more person I was going to have the pleasure of tossing out the door.

I stormed back inside and yelled to the staff "Who is waiting on the drunk bitch and her soon to be very embarrassed husband?"

To my chagrin I had an instant response from one of the waiters. I was hoping to have to do a little more investigating because that would mean there were no signs of a problem before this.

The waiter who happened to speak up was Kevin. Kevin is not a big fan of confrontation. Kevin also realizes that his tip is contingent on the customer having a pleasant experience from the beginning to the end of their time at the cinema pub. But, what Kevin realizes the most is that I don't put up with any bullshit. So if he had told me about a problem than that pleasant experience was not going to be a reality.

"Kevin" I began, trying to control my anger "Go to the table and tell Betsy Wetsy's husband that it is time to pay the bill and get the hell out. Tell him he doesn't have to go home but I would suggest someplace with port-o-lets. Now Kevin!"

As I mentioned earlier Kevin doesn't like confrontation. These instructions made him very hesitant but he knew he would rather deal with Mr. Wetsy than with me. About three minutes later, Kevin returns from the cinema and tells me that the husband did not seem surprised he was being asked to leave.

"Obviously, not the first time" I say "is he paying the bill and leaving?"

"Well" Kevin says "He just wants to finish his beer first."

"Are you fucking kidding me Kevin?" I scream. "Get back in there and tell that fucking sheep to grab his wife's box of depends and take her back to the trailer before I have to go in there myself and make this situation even worse than it already is."

Kevin unwillingly walked back into the cinema and to be honest, I didn't have much faith in him. But about thirty seconds later the poor bastard that is married to this train wreck walked out with his head down. He went outside and grabbed his wife who at this point had been out there for fifteen minutes (I guess he really missed her). I could hear her trying to explain herself as they walked to their car.

"Kevin, he paid the bill I hope." I said.

"Yes, he actually left me a twenty dollar tip." He answered with a big smile.

"Glad I could help." I say as I walk away in disgust.

And so began the bullshit that I was to endure on a nightly basis. Luckily though, it was the last time I had to throw a pair of urine soaked shoes away. Unfortunately those were my favorite shoes.

Quickie # 1

Everybody Enjoys a Quickie

Dumb customer: "Can I order a Budweiser please?"

Me: "Sure, I just need to see an ID please."

Dumb Customer: "I didn't drive so I don't have my license with me. Why, do I not look old look old enough to you?"

Me: "Of course you look old enough Regis. I really just wanted to see your address so I knew where the next MENSA meeting was being held."

Dumb Customer: "My name isn't Regis (Wow, really) and I have no idea what MENSA is (Not a shocker). Like I said though, I didn't drive so I don't have my license with me. I can assure you that I am old enough to order a beer."

Me: "Your assurances are not what I am looking for. I'm looking for proof, but I will give you another option. I'm going to ask you three questions and if you answer all three correctly not only will I serve you that beer, I will pay for the first one."

Dumb Customer: "It's a deal."

Me: "No shit it's a deal Howie Mendel. You really have no other option. So, my first question is do I look stupid to you?"

Dumb Customer: "I'm thinking I should say no."

Me: "Good answer Regis. Now my second question is do you have your wallet with you?"

Dumb Customer: "I still don't know who Regis is (Is this fucking guy serious?) but, the answer is yes. I always have my wallet with me."

Me: "Wow, you're two for two. Just one more correct answer and you have yourself a free beer. Last question: Where do you keep your license?"

Dumb Customer: "Can I get a Coke please?"

Me: "Coming right up Regis and thank you for playing."

Chapter 3

Bad Boys, Bad Boys, Whatcha Gonna Do

It's a beautiful Sunday afternoon in the middle of the summertime. Not a cloud in the sky and the cinema pub is pretty slow. I'm able to watch most of the Red Sox game without any interruptions. What could possibly go wrong today? Why did I have to ask?

One of the waitresses comes into the kitchen and informs me that one of her customers is yelling at her husband and refuses to stop.

I say to the waitress "Tell her if she does not quiet down she will be asked to leave. If she has a problem with that than she can come out here to the lobby and I will explain the situation to her."

Now, whenever I ask one of my employees to "talk" to a problem customer, I always go into the cinema, stand in the back, and watch the reaction of the customer. To my absolute amazement this crazy bitch started punching her husband (poor bastard in need of a lawyer) and screaming at him.

"Time for me to get involved." I say to myself as I walk towards Mrs. Whitetrash 1975.

"Could I talk to you in the lobby please?" I ask in a very pleasant tone.

"Fuck you." Was the response I received.

"Now this is not a request." I snapped back very unpleasantly this time. "Out! In the lobby now."

As this poster child for birth control followed me to the lobby she screamed every obscenity you could ever think of at me. Some of them I had never even heard before. Pretty impressive considering I think of myself as an expert in that field. More importantly though, in my mind now, it was on. Gloves off bitch. No holds barred.

"In case you haven't noticed, we're not filming an episode of COPS here today." I started with. "If you want to have a domestic disturbance you can do it somewhere else. I will not allow it here."

"Fuck you asshole." She snapped back. "The problems between me and my husband are none of your business."

"Wrong again you festering boil on the ass of all that is human." I shot back with trying to figure out where I pulled that one out of. "As soon as you brought those problems in here you made it my business. Now it is time for you and that poor excuse of a man you call your husband to get the fuck out."

I started to walk away thinking it was over. Hoping she would just grab her husband by the scruff of his neck and drag him back to the dungeon. As always I was sorely mistaken.

"Maybe the reason you are so slow today." I hear her say. "Is because you are an asshole."

I thought about what she said for five minutes (seconds) before I turned around and responded with "The main reason we are slow today bitch is the fact that it's eighty degrees and sunny. Now, I know you are not smart enough to figure it out on your own, but on nice days like today, people tend to spend their time doing outdoor activities. You, on the other hand like to be in dark places because there is not enough sunshine in the universe to make you look any better than Joseph Merrick on a good day. Another reason we might be slow." I continued. "Ignorant assholes like you make it difficult for decent people with all their teeth to enjoy a movie without a Jerry Springer episode breaking out in the cinema. Now get the hell out of here before the situation gets any uglier. I realize that with you involved it is hard to believe it can get any uglier considering you have cornered the ugly market. But I assure you it can."

To my amazement, this Gwendolyn Graham (look it up) wannabe had no response whatsoever. She walked out the door and was never seen again (until The National Enquirer published the photos of Big Foot spotted in the mountains of South Dakota).

"The husband?" I ask the dumbfounded (basically just dumb) waitress.

"He is hiding in the corner but he will be out any second." She informs me.

Before I can get any more pissed off, this poor bastard walks out of the cinema. He looks like a seventy five year old retiree with a metal detector on the beaches of Cape Cod. His head is facing straight down at the ground and nothing is going to make him look up. The only thing missing are the black socks and sandals.

"I left the money on the table." He mumbled as he walked out the door. "Keep the change."

For a moment I actually felt bad for the poor bastard. I can assure you though, that moment didn't last very long.

Quickie # 2

Dumb Customer: "Can we bring in Chinese food from the restaurant next door?"

Me: "Do I look Chinese?"

Dumb Customer: "No, not at all."

Me: "That was a rhetorical question dumbass. The answer is no."

Dumb Customer: "I don't see why not?"

Me: "Well then Mr. Magoo, I suggest you get some new glasses. We sell food here so why would it make any sense to allow you bring in food from another establishment ?"

Dumb Customer: "So, it is all about the money to you ?"

Me: "Do you have a job?"

Dumb Customer: "Of course I do."

Me: "Not the answer I expected, but I will take your word for it. Why do you have a job?"

Adam Ballarino

Dumb Customer: "So I can pay my bills and have money to live day to day."

Me: "My point exactly shithead. Now, if you have any other questions, you can reach me at <u>WWW.FUCKOFF.COM</u>. I don't look forward to hearing from you."

Chapter 4

I'm an Asshole

I'm sure that most of you that have made it this far are saying to yourselves "Wow, this guy sounds like a real asshole. He talks about and treats people like shit."

You would be correct in some of your observations. You would also be someone that most likely never worked in the food service industry. I would like to think those of you that have been in the business can see where I am coming from. There is a difference between the food service industry and other service industries.

Understand that I am not trying to make excuses for my behavior. I don't feel I need to excuse anything I have done. I offer no apologies for any of my actions when it relates to my time in the worst of all possible professions. My point is simply that even the kindest person in the world (Me) can morph into an absolute asshole (Me) when subjected to an abundance of disrespect, arrogance, ignorance, and self entitlement on a daily basis.

The simple fact that I might be the unfortunate person that greeted you at the door as you walked in does not mean I am responsible for all that is wrong with your life. I'm here to do a job just like you are when you go to work every day. Would you want me to show up at your workplace and take my frustrations out on you for no other reason than the fact that you are there? Let me answer that one for you. NO.

I guess what I am trying to say is (Hell, at this point I don't even know where this is going.) there are no occupations I can think of that don't involve some kind of service. But for some reason unknown to me it is accepted to treat food service employees as second class citizens. Though, I have some theories.

One theory I have is that some people might treat each time out as a one and done event. Please let me do my best to explain. The following is my attempt to get into the mind of a complete asshole.

I've had a shitty day, a shitty week, a shitty month, hell, my whole life is shitty. Wait a minute. I have a great idea. I am going to go out and make somebody else feel as shitty as I do. That should make me feel so much better. Treat someone else like shit and we're all even. Even if I do go back to the same place again I'll probably have another server. If I have the same server, there's no way they remember me. One and done.

These complete assholes would be wrong. Anyone that has lasted more than two weeks in this business will tell you that they can remember the face of the soccer mom from two years ago that left a $3 tip on a $40 tab. They might not be able to remember the specials of the day but they can recall the exact percentage they received on every bill for the last ten years.

STOP! I CAN'T DO THIS ANY MORE.

The last eight paragraphs you read is a bunch of bullshit. The only reason I even started writing all that crap is the fact I finally let my wife read what I had written. She said she was horrified with the way it made me look as a person. She said I needed to tone it down and make myself look more sympathetic.

So I started writing what I finally realized was some sort of disclaimer.

"ADAM IS NOT AN ASSHOLE. HE IS MERELY A VICTIM OF CIRCUMSTANCE. WHAT HE SAYS DOES NOT EXPRESS THE THOUGHTS THAT ARE ACTUALLY IN HIS HEAD"

Fuck that. I can't lie. I'm pissed at myself for wasting the time to defend the actual people who made me this jaded. No offense to my wife. I love her dearly but she wasn't there when I was called a fucking moron for not accepting a coupon from "Showcase Cinemas".

It is not my fault that you either can't read or follow directions. Maybe you can't read and you can't follow directions. Whatever the case may be, do not use me as your doormat. You might think trying to make me miserable is going to make you feel better, but I assure you that in the long run you are the one who will lose.

If you still feel that I am an asshole than I can't change that. I tried to make myself the victim but I am not a victim. I' m not a victim because I never let myself be one. I fought fire with fire, which in my case meant being a bigger asshole than the asshole who started the fight.

If you don't like the way I think than there is a simple solution. Stop reading. That's what dealing with the public has turned me into. A complete asshole. When in Rome.

Everything I have written is exactly the way I feel. I refuse to sugarcoat anything that I have done or said up to this point or that I may say or do in the future. What you see is what you get. The fact that it might be a while before my wife will be seen in public with me again cannot sway me into altering the truth. Sorry honey, but in the words of the immortal Bill Belichick "It is what it is."

So there you go. The disclaimer is retracted. If you wish to keep reading, please continue. If not, go back to your reruns of "Wife Swap". Either way it doesn't matter to me. I'm not trying to sell books (the publisher will love that line.) I'm trying to educate the public on an epidemic that threatens our very way of life. PURE FUCKING IGNORANCE AND STUPIDITY.

Wow, I feel so much better all of a sudden. Now, where was I?

Quickie #3

Dumb Customer: "I have to use the bathroom. Could you please pause the movie? I don't want to miss anything."

Me: "No I can't pause the movie. You are not sitting on the couch in your living room. There are other customers in the theater watching the movie and they don't care about your weak bladder."

Dumb Customer: "Well that's just stupid. What am I supposed to do about the parts of the movie I miss while I'm in the bathroom?"

Me: "Depends."

Dumb Customer: "Depends on what?"

Me: "You misunderstood. What I meant was you need to wear Depends to avoid these situations. Seriously though, my concern is not about the parts of the movie you are going to miss. My concern is how I get the last five minutes of my life spent talking to you back."

Chapter 5

Bruschetta Biiiiiiiiitch

The most infamous customer we have is universally (within the walls of the cinema pub) known as "The Bruschetta Bitch". For the purposes of this book I will just refer to her as BB. There are two factors that led to us referring to her with that moniker.

The first reason is that the only thing she has ever ordered besides an ice water with extra lemon (you know who you are assholes) is the Bruschetta pizza. The second reason is that she is pure and simply a bitch. I tried for a little while to give her the benefit of the doubt. Everybody has bad days. Everybody has bad weeks. I finally realized that was not the case with this woman. She talked to us "little people" with the same tone as Leona Helmsey talked to her accountant when she said to him "Yes, the dog gets everything."

This woman was Aileen Wournos (look it up) on a good day. She is approximately fifty years old with teeth so nasty it would take a sandblaster, a jackhammer, and a hazmat suit just to make her look human. She looks like she fell out of the ugly tree and hit every branch on the way down. She looks like God was beating her with the ugly stick and when the stick broke he started kicking her. I could go on forever but I think you get the point. Susan Boyle looks like a supermodel compared to this bitch. Alright, that's my last one.

What you need to realize about this festering boil on the ass of all that is human, is by her own admission she has tried and failed numerous times to make the Bruschetta pizza at home (her cage at the zoo). The only reason she comes in is for that pizza. Who would have ever thought that being good at something could come back to bite you in the ass.

Every time this *%#$@ comes in she licks her plate clean and then complains that the pizza was burnt. I've told her that without any evidence I can't confirm her story. I've also told her at least four times to never come back again. Unfortunately she listens about as well as she brushes her teeth. Not very often and not very well.

One night she told me she wanted the pizza taken off her bill and I said "Absolutely fucking not."

"I'm going to call Sam." she threatened "And you'll be in big fucking trouble."

Sam is the owner of the Cinema Pub. He is also my brother. He also had one experience with this bitch and told me I could get a restraining order against her if I wanted to. The only reason I didn't is because it would eliminate the fun I have when I get to embarrass this piece of shit.

"How long have you known Sam?" I ask with a big shit eating grin on my face.

"Twenty fucking years you asshole." she spouted. "And tomorrow you will be out of a job."

I wish they could all serve me up softballs right down the middle of the plate like this fucking bag of smashed assholes just did. I don't even have to try to embarrass her. It is just going to flow at this point.

"Well" I said "If I'm out of a job then I guess that means you and I will have something in common other than the fact that we both look like men."

"You better not talk to me like that." she warned.

"Maybe you were not paying attention." I said "Your threats don't bother me. As a matter of fact just give me a second to get the phone. I'll dial Sam's number because I am positive that you don't have it but I'll let you talk to your old friend and we'll see how this situation ends."

"I have his number you fucking pissant." she so eloquently responded. "I'll call him myself."

I stood there for a good two, or three minutes, and watched this crazy bitch have a fake conversation with my brother. If I wasn't so mesmerized by the hilarity of the situation I would have called my brother myself so he could enjoy this moment with me. Unfortunately all that was going through my mind was one question. Why the fuck does this nonstop menstrual cycle have a cell phone?

There is no fucking way on Earth that this colostomy bag with a pulse has any friends. Her family probably staged their own death years ago just to get the fuck away from her. Maybe it was a direct line to the devil himself. No, that can't be, even Lucifer (that's what us friends call him) has standards and this bitch would make even him blush. Finally I had to put a stop to the bullshit.

"Hey, shit for brains, what did my brother say?" I asked "Did I lose my job or do I still have the authority to tell you to Get The Fuck Out. Oh, I'm sorry, please Get The Fuck Out."

It took her about three minutes to realize what I had just said.

"Sam is your brother?" she mumbled. "No, you're lying."

"Really? You all knowing ogre." I began. "Tell me. What is your BFF, Sam's, last name? If you know him so well, then you must surely know that?"

"I don't need to prove anything to you." she proclaimed.

"Ah, but you did just prove something to me." I responded. "You proved that you are a liar and a miserable, ignorant bitch. You also proved what I had expected all along—that you are even stupider than you are ugly. That's a pretty big feat considering that you make Roseanne Barr look like the Prom Queen."

"I've had enough of your insults." she screamed. "I'm never coming here again."

"I wish I could believe you." I said sincerely. "But unfortunately, you and I both know that is not the truth. The fact of the matter is that until you can reach the intelligence level of a mentally handicapped farm animal and learn how to put six simple ingredients together to successfully make a fucking pizza you will be back. That is my harsh reality to live with. Although I do enjoy these witty little diatribes we have with each other. One sided as they may be."

With that she stormed out the door never to be seen again. Seriously though, do you really think I am that lucky ? There is more to be told about this fucking perfect case for the death penalty.

Not even a week later this butt plug with semi normal motor function (sorry, I'm running out of ways to accurately describe this crazy bitch.) is in again to see a movie and have her cherished of all meals. She walks in like nothing has ever happened and asks for one ticket to any movie that is showing.

"Nice to see you too." I say as sarcastically as possible. "You're water and pizza will be there as soon as I determine whether or not I want you to stay."

"Sounds good." She says oblivious to the fact that I might not actually serve her anything.

Now, anybody that is still reading this realizes that I have to serve this asshole. It is assuring that I have a story for the night. I have grown to love shoving it back up the ass of the people who (or whom, I'm not sure about this one.) are trying to shove it up mine. I figure I can have some fun.

For the second time in my life I was wrong. (The first was when I bought the Betamax instead of the VHS. Who could have known?) This bitch actually walked out without paying her bill. I thought about it for two seconds and came to the conclusion that nobody would skip out on a bill and come back to the same place. This actually would be great for me. All it took to be rid of this bitch was a free pizza. If I had known that I would have delivered a pizza to her cage every week.

AGAIN, I was wrong. Now I am pissed. I've been wrong three times in my life and this bitch is the center of focus on two of those occasions.

Let me explain. The very next day after she walked out on her tab she showed up at the front door knocking to get in. We weren't open yet but I happened to be walking through the lobby and notice the zombie like figure outside. Again, wrongly thinking that she realized she walked out without paying and she was there to make good on her debt. As I unlocked the door I noticed she had a twenty dollar bill in her hand.

"You realized you didn't pay your tab last night?" I ask as I grab the twenty out of her claw.

"No." She grunts "I just want to get a ticket for tonight's 6:45 show."

"Sorry." I say as I close the door in her face. "We don't sell tickets in advance."

As I walked away I heard her pounding on the door. I waited about fifteen minutes before I went back in the lobby and saw that she was still standing outside the door.

"Can I help you?" I asked as if I didn't even know her.

"I wanted to see a movie tonight and you just took my last twenty dollars." She said. "What am I supposed to do now?"

"That really isn't my problem." I said as the wheels in my head began to spin. "Maybe you could find another house to haunt. Perhaps there is a village out there looking for an idiot. You would be perfect for that role. If they're making another Shrek movie you could be a body double. The Pro-Choice people might be looking for evidence in their favor. A PSA from you would cement their position on the topic. I have to go back to work now, so, you'll excuse me if I shut this door in your face and walk away."

Believe it or not she came back. I have a journal filled with stories about this bitch. Maybe someday I will share more. I just need my therapist to sign off.

Quickie #4

Dumb Customer: "You're going to charge me a 15% gratuity just because I have 8 people in my party?"

Me: "That's what the sign says."

Dumb Customer: "That is unbelievable."

Me: "What's unbelievable is the fact that you found 7 people that would be seen in public with you."

Dumb Customer: "I'll pay it but this will be the last time."

Me: "I can only dream."

Chapter 6

Racist Bastards

Most of the things I have seen and heard over the years I can eventually look back on and laugh. Most of them I will just write off to pure stupidity, ignorance, or just a general knowledge about how the normal people in this world act.

Unfortunately, this next story still pisses me off to this very day. It is about a couple that thought they were higher on the food chain than the rest of us common folk. That part of their personality I have to deal with. I deal with assholes like these two every day. It's in my job description. Another personality trait that they exhibited, though, is not one I have to put up with. As a matter of fact I refuse to put up with it.

They were racist motherfuckers and that is something I will not tolerate. I have no patience for small minded people when it comes to topics such as this. I don't know if I dealt with the situation in the best way that I could have. I also don't care if I dealt with the situation the best way I could have.

It's a very busy Friday night and we're just getting into the heart of the rush. I'm trying to do ten things at once when I hear a waitress call my name.

"Adam" she says. "There is a couple in the cove that wanted me to tell you that they don't like the background music."

I laugh this off thinking it is one of my friends just busting my balls. Boy was I wrong. Five minutes later the same waitress comes in the kitchen and informs me that this same couple would like to discuss the music choices with me. Not only do I not have the time to deal with this bullshit, I definitely don't have the patience. I realize though that I have to address this before it goes too far.

I start walking to the theater with one part of my brain telling me to rip into these two right from the get go. The other half is telling me to be calm and cool and handle it like a professional. I listened to the latter and I can assure you that it will never happen again.

Me: "Is there a problem here?"

Racist Douchebag: "Yes, there is a problem. I don't like this music."

Me: "I don't like paying taxes but short of a flat out Ruby Ridge thing there is nothing I can do about it. Is there anything else?"

Racist Dickhead: "My wife just told you she doesn't like the music. What are you going to do about it?"

Me: "Turn it up louder. No, seriously though, we have had the same discs in for a year now and nobody has ever complained."

Racist Dickhead: "Consider this your first complaint then. My wife just got out of work and she just wants to relax. This music is keeping her from doing that."

Me: "REAAAAAAALLLLLY? I got to work at 8:00 AM this morning and will not be leaving until midnight at the earliest. So you will forgive me if I have no sympathy for bitchzilla here. I understand that the job as a freak show in a traveling circus is seasonal but she made that decision. Now before I walk away never to think of you two assholes again, what is wrong with the music?"

Racist Douchebag: "It sounds like a bunch of jigaboos running around and screaming."

Why didn't I just walk away before I asked that question? Because I am a glutton for punishment is all I can think of. The reason I asked is not important at this point. The answer to the question is paramount. The answer I received, had me so infuriated that I was almost at a loss for words. Almost!

"Did you just use the word jigaboo?" I ask in pure amazement. "Never mind, I know the answer. I also know that that is the most offensive, reprehensible, and utterly disgusting thing I have ever heard."

At this point I realize that my voice was raised to a point that the other customers could hear everything that I was saying. Normally I wouldn't want to have a confrontation in front of other customers but on this most special of occasions I wanted everybody else to know just what kind of scumbags these two assholes were. What made it even better was that I could sense that those people who were unfortunate enough to hear the beginning of this exchange were on my side. I even got the sense that a couple of them wanted to join in. I decided I should just end it before it escalated any further.

"This is what is going to happen now." I started. "For the sake of everyone involved, including my anger management councilor, you two ballbags are going to get up and walk out to the lobby very quietly. I will then, very reluctantly, return your ticket money. Then you will walk out the door and never be seen here again. Failure to comply with those instructions will result in permanent physical and emotional damage to you and probably jail time for me. Oh, but it will be well worth it. Okay then let's go."

Luckily enough they complied with what I thought was an extremely fair settlement to this most unfortunate of all incidents. If they hadn't I don't know what I would have said or done next. I probably would have had to finish writing this on the prison library typewriter with my cellmate Bubba serving as my spell check.

As they walked out I couldn't resist one last shot. "Have a good night assholes." I said "Maybe there is a clan meeting you could get to. Tell all the good old boys I said hey. By the way, David Duke can kiss my ass."

As busy as it was, I had to go outside for a couple of minutes to calm down. I sat down and tried to rationalize what someone could be thinking when spoke those words to a complete stranger. The only answer I could come up with is what has become my standard go to. They are just ignorant fucking assholes.

Quickie #5

Dumb Customer: "This is our first time here. Are we going to see live actors?"

Me: "If me acting sincere when I tell you that's not the first time I've been asked that stupid question counts then the answer to your stupid question would be yes."

Chapter 7

Sorry, I Don't Know the Score

I am a huge sports fan. Being from Boston, I live and die with the Patriots and Red Sox. I love the Celtics and Bruins as well. In the time since the cinema has opened I have been fortunate enough to see the Patriots win three Super Bowls, the Red Sox two World Series, the Celtics another NBA Championship, and the Bruins, well nothing yet from the Bruins. The thing that always drove me crazy was to have to work when there was a big game on. Don't get me wrong, we do have a T.V. in the kitchen and a satellite dish, but it is not the same as watching with friends and going nuts on every play. I understand that I should be happy with any business we might get on these occasions but quite simply I am not.

The reason I hate it isn't because I can't concentrate on the game. The main reason is that everybody that happens to come in on these nights feels the need to remind me how much it must suck that I am working during the Big Game. To those assholes (you know who you are) I say "Fuck you. I have no choice but to be here. You do. So either stay home or shut the fuck up."

Anyway, here are a couple of stories related to this subject:

Story 1:

A couple walks in and buys two tickets to "The Sisterhood of the Traveling Pants." It just happens to be the same night the Red Sox face elimination from playoffs. I will grant the husband that no one expected the Sox to come back from three games down against the Yankees to win the series and eventually the World Series for the first time since Larry King married his first wife. My point is simply to grow a set. The fucking pants will still be traveling tomorrow.

Now, I really did feel bad for this poor bastard. Not only for missing the game, but for having to sit through this painfully bad excuse of a movie. My pity for him, however, was outweighed by the fact that he let it happen.

About thirty minutes later I saw my opportunity to relay my feelings to him in a very discreet way. A way I could have fun with and hope that in the end he got my message.

I looked out the kitchen window into the lobby and saw him looking around like a child that had gotten separated from their mother in a supermarket.

"Let the good times start." I thought to myself as I walked to the lobby and asked "Is there something I can help you with?"

"I told my wife I needed to go to the bathroom." he whispered "But I really just want to know the score of the game. Are you watching? What is the score? Are the Sox winning? What is going on?"

"Take a breath." I said with the wheels in my head spinning. "First of all, there is no need to whisper. The cinema walls are sound proof. She can't hear you." I continued, trying to put him at ease before I could lay this next load of bullshit on him. "I don't know exactly which game you are referring to. I'm actually watching old episodes of Dr. Who on PBS. It is very interesting stuff. I've already seen this episode but it's just as good the second time around."

He looked at me with the blank stare of Ray Charles trying to pick a suspect out of a police lineup. It took about three minutes but he eventual spoke again.

"DR. WHO?" he questioned "I was talking about the Red Sox game. You do know they are playing the Yankees right now don't you?"

"I am sorry sir." I answered with a slight hint of sarcasm. "But, I don't follow basketball."

"Its baseball!" he screamed "The fucking playoffs!"

"Again, I am sorry but I don't know what you are talking about." I said with a completely straight face that should have earned me an Oscar nomination. "Now if you don't mind, I would like to get back to my show. You enjoy the rest of the pants movie."

I had to run back into the kitchen so I would not burst into laughter right in front of him. I also wanted to know what the score of the game was. Once I composed myself I took a quick peek in the lobby to see if he was still there. He was on his cell phone and I could hear him asking the person on the other end to fill him in on the details of the game.

I decided that this was the perfect time to drive my macho point home. I ran back into the lobby and in my best impression of an excited school girl I asked "Did you get the score? Are we winning?"

"David Ortiz just hit" he began and then stopped. He thought for a minute and then asked "You know what just happened don't you? You knew all along. Point taken."

I just smiled and walked back into the kitchen. When the movie ended, I watched him sprint out the door dragging his wife behind him. The last words I heard come from his mouth were "Never again."

Story 2:

This story is also sports related. The difference is that the circumstances didn't lean towards me in a humorous (fuck with the customer) type of mood. It was basically pure spite on my part. Although I feel it was justified, you can make your own judgment. If you agree with me, then great. If you don't agree with me, then you can go shit in a hat because you are probably the type of person I am writing about. Anyway, before I offend anybody else, here is the next story.

I normally don't work on Sundays but this particular Sunday my friend Jaoan asked if I could cover for him. The reason I needed to cover for Jaoan was that he was flying to Houston to try and get tickets for the Super Bowl. The Super Bowl that had the Patriots playing in it. The only reason I agreed to this was that Jaoan had helped me out many times in the past when I needed time off. I also figured that nobody in Massachusetts would be going to the movies while the Pats were in the Super Bowl. I was wrong. There were two people in Massachusetts that would be going to the movies on this night and I was lucky enough to working in the theater that they had chosen.

Its 6:30pm and the introductions are just starting. There are no customers yet, so I figure I'll be on my way by kickoff. WRONG!

These two women (Biiiiiiitches) walk through the door wearing of all things Patriots jerseys. They want to see a movie. Isn't that special for me.

I politely ask "You young ladies (middle aged douchebags) don't want to see the big game?"

"Oh no." the skinny one (she's the one that could see her shoes) responded. "Every time we watch the Patriots they lose."

"In other words," I thought to myself, "Your husbands want you out of the house so they can enjoy the game and I can be pushed to the brink of suicide."

Then Orca #1 has the nerve to ask "You will keep us updated on the score though?"

"No" I answered with enough hatred in my heart to make Hitler blush. "There will be no updates on the score."

"I don't understand. Why not?" inquired Orca #2.

"You are here to watch a movie. Do I have that right?" were the words I could not stop from angrily spewing out of my mouth.

"Well yes" answered #1 "but we also want to know if the Patriots are winning."

"Lady, you don't know the difference between a screen pass and a screen door. The only reason you want to know the score is so you can judge what kind of mood your poor husbands are going to be in when you get home."

I was losing it now. "But I am happy to take one for the team tonight and let him have his four hours a year away from you. I feel like I am donating to charity. I should be able to write this off on my taxes. They say no good deed goes unpunished. I must have done a lot of good deeds to deserve this. Go watch your movie and leave me alone to slit my wrists."

This probably was not my finest moment, but I felt better when I was done and the Patriots ended up winning the Super Bowl. All's well that ends well.

Since the time I initially wrote these two stories, the Bruins won The Stanley Cup. I was able to enjoy the entire series either at home or out with friends. Just one of many perks that come from the smartest decision in my life—Quitting the food service business.

Quickie #6

Dumb Customer: "You aren't advertising the movie we want to see. Would it be possible to show the movie we want to see?"

Me: "Of course it would be."

Dumb Customer: "Great, where do we go?"

Me: "The entertainment section of your local newspaper."

Chapter 8

Wrong Cinema Pub Asshole

My friend and coworker Jaoan and I worked the same function every year. It's for these four very nice women who bring about forty or so Middle School students to watch a movie and have brunch. This one particular year turned out to be a little different than normal.

We had just finished serving brunch when this complete numbnut knocked on the door with 8 ten year old boys and a VCR tape. This is the exchanged that followed.

Me: "Can I help you sir?"

Numbnut: "I booked a birthday party for 11:30am today."

Me: "I think you might be mistaken. We do not have any birthday parties booked for today."

Numbnut: "I AM NOT mistaken. My wife booked this party for here today and I expect it to begin immediately."

At this point, I realize that not only does this idiot have the wrong information but that he is not too happy about having to spend this time with his own son, never mind his son's friends. I also realized that he was full of shit. He first told me that he had booked the party himself, but when questioned about it, he told me his wife had booked it. I now realize it's time to have some fun with this moron.

Me: "Sir, you are mistaken. Now if you just tell me who you talked to I'm sure we can figure this mess out."

Numbnut: "There is nothing to figure out. You forgot about my son's birthday party, and now I expect you to fix it."

I know for a fact that he is wrong, but I now want to drag this out as long as possible to get the full entertainment value of it.

Me: "I didn't forget your son's birthday. I didn't even know it was his birthday. You must understand I have never even met your son. I'm sure he's a very fine young man, but you have yet to even introduce us. Realistically, I could not possibly forget something that I never had knowledge of. None the less, if you could just tell me which movie you thought you would be viewing today maybe we could resolve this like two grownups."

Numbnut: "The movie on this video that I was told to bring, so you could show it on the big screen."

This is getting better by the second. This fucking guy is a bigger moron than I thought he was.

Me: "Well, I am sorry to inform you SIR but we do not have a VCR. We don't even have a T.V." (We do have a T.V., but it is in the kitchen.)

Numbnut: "Well, I talked to the owner's wife and daughter, and both of them told me to bring a tape of the movie that the kids wanted to see."

With every word he speaks, he exceeds even my expectations of how absolutely fucking stupid he really is. But now the fun for me is starting to fade and I am starting to get very annoyed. Time to end this.

Me:	"Now you are just proving how totally wrong you are. First, you said you booked this party. Then you said your wife booked it. Now, it's back to you again. Only this time, you say that you talked to the owner's wife and his daughter. Well, I am sorry to inform you. No, wait a second. I am not sorry to inform you. I am just simply going to inform you that the owner does not have a daughter and his wife has nothing to do with this establishment. Now, if you give me the name and phone number of this mystery person you claim you or your wife spoke to maybe we can sort out what actually happened here."
Numbnut:	"I don't have the number with me (big fucking surprise!). And it was a real person, not a mystery person. And the only way this gets resolved is for you to give my son the party he was promised."

At this point he is yelling and screaming. Unfortunately, the four nice women from the real party are all witnessing this fucking moron unraveling right in front of them. It is time for me to stop being nice.

Me:	"You listen to me for a second asshole. Keep your fucking voice down before I rip your voice box out. Go outside and call your wife. See if she can explain how you fucked up a task so simple that Courtney Love in a relapse could have pulled it off. Then as a favor to me, go play in traffic. But don't try blaming this one on anybody but yourself."

Angrily, he stomps outside dialing his phone. I watched him the whole time. He was flailing his arms and stomping the ground like Paris Hilton being denied entry to a club. All I could hear was screaming. I couldn't actually make out any words. Then it happened. It was the sign of defeat and I loved it. He put his hand on his forehead and looked directly down at the ground. The yelling stopped and he hung up the phone. He then looked back up at the sky in utter defeat and held that pose for about two minutes.

He finally made his way back inside with his tail between his legs knowing that he had just made a complete ass of himself. I just had to get one more jab in.

Me: "Do you have a confirmation number or something so we can put an end to this mess?"

Numbnut: "Actually, I have the wrong place."

Me: "Really? I can't believe that. All this time, I was thinking that I was at fault. Wow, now what are you going to do with these boys for the next three hours? Actually, I have a better question. Where are you supposed to be?"

Numbnut: "Some place in Connecticut."

Are you kidding me! I was in the midst of calling this jackass every name in the book when I was interrupted by one of the women from the Middle School. She actually invited him to stay with the boys and watch the movie with their party. She even let them eat everything that was left from the buffet.

This dickhead was lucky enough to turn a disaster into a decent birthday for his kid without even trying. And it didn't cost him anything. The women got a thank you and a big hug. I didn't even get an apology for all the shit I had to put up with. I had to sit there with my mouth shut and watch them enjoy themselves.

It just goes to show you that although it doesn't always pay to be nice, apparently, it pays to be a douchebag.

Quickie #7

Dumb Customer: "Can I order the mozzarella sticks with the cheese on the side?"

Me: I just walked away shaking my head without saying a word.

Chapter 9

Urination Deja Vu

You may remember reading earlier about the drunk bitch that relieved herself (pissed) on my shoes. This story, although not quite as bad (no purchase of new shoes required) is along the same lines.

    I'm outside enjoying some "me time" after two hours of utter chaos, when I notice someone out of the corner my eye. Fortunately for me, or not, this asshole does not see me as I stand on the loading dock staring down on this shithead waiting to see what happens next. At this point in my food service career, I had decided that if there was no immediate danger to me or my employees then I would let things develop a little more before I react. I deserve some amusement for the shit I have to endure on a nightly basis and I know with this guy I can really make this fun. I just didn't anticipate what was actually going to happen.

    He unrolled the sleeve of his t-shirt to get to his pack of cigs (I love that reference from The Outsiders), lit his cigarette, unzipped his pants, and began to piss on the loading dock. He let out a sigh of relief as though it had been days since he last urinated. My time to act.

    "You do realize that we have restrooms inside the building don't you?" I ask in a tone that is just loud enough to surprise him to the level of pissing all over the front of his pants.

It took a couple of minutes for him to put his unit away, clean himself off, and realize where the voice he heard was coming from. Apparently, he did not use those couple of minutes to come up with an answer that was acceptable to me.

"Yes I do." he said as he dried his hands on his shirt. "But you can't smoke in there."

Maybe my brain doesn't work the same as most people but this response made no sense to me whatsoever. So after a couple of seconds of trying to decipher the code in which I assumed he was speaking, I calculated that there was no such code. He was just plain old stupid. I was correct to let this get to the point where I could have some fun. This guy was right in my wheelhouse.

"Does the nicotine help with the urine flow?" I ask in a very condescending way. "Or is it the glowing red ember that close to your dick that makes it work for you? I'm just curious."

"You can't talk to me like that." he said. "I'm a customer."

"Oh, I'm sorry Tweedle Dumbest" I responded. "You must not have gotten the memo."

"Memo, what memo?" he asked.

"The one that said Fuck You!" I embarrassingly screamed.

As I walked back inside hoping this was over (knowing it wasn't). I heard him muttering under his horribly bad breath that I was unprofessional (maybe a valid point.), and that he wouldn't stand for it. So I waited for him in the lobby, knowing this dickhead was outside rehearsing exactly what he was going to say to me when he came back inside. The only variable, was how long it would take him to devise a reputable defense for his pissing in public offense.

No one will ever know the answer to that because when he finally returned he had no excuse for his lewd and lascivious act—an act that with the help of a camera phone would put him on the sex offender list at the very least. Instead, he decided to verbally come after me.

"You should never have talked to me like that." his rant began. "It was extremely rude."

"Could you spell extremely for me?" I asked in an obvious mocking tone.

"Spell what ?" he responded.

"I'll take that as a no." I start with. "And the only rude thing that happened here tonight was you treating the outside of this building as your own personal fire hydrant. If you can't take a leak without a cigarette burning in your hand than you should call Dr. Phil and get a referral for somebody who deals with really fucked up people like yourself."

"I will not stand for this." he said very forcefully.

"Fine." I responded. "Then sit the fuck down, take it all in, and I hope to never see you again. Now, I have work to do. I understand that the word work is not in your vocabulary but when your vocabulary is limited to twenty "words", I guess meth and tweaking take priority. I have to go now. Be careful not to blow yourself up you fucking felony waiting to happen."

As I walked away, I realized I could have handled myself better but I was done letting people piss all over me. (pun intended.)

Quickie #8

Dumb Customer: "I know we are late. Can you rewind to the beginning of the movie?"

Me: "Of course I can."

Dumb Customer: "Great, we'll take two tickets please."

Me: "That's hilarious, I was just kidding. Next time learn how to read a clock."

Chapter 10

Thanks for Your Concern Officer

The cops in the town that the cinema is located in are widely known to try to and look like hard ass'. This next story is just one more example of that fact. Now, on a normal weekday I would not get to the cinema until between three or four in the afternoon. On this particular occasion though, I had gotten a call from a delivery driver at about noon that he was on his way with a food shipment. I gave all the drivers my number for days just like this when they may be running ahead of schedule.

"That's fine." I tell him. "I am on my way."

The only problem was that I was in the process of selling my condo and there were real estate agents showing up with possible buyers all the time without notice. The only reason this was a problem was that I have a dog and could not leave him home knowing that if someone showed up it might cause a problem. So I took him with me like I had done a hundred times before. Never did I think it would almost land me in jail.

I arrive at the cinema just as the driver was pulling in. I knew it would only take him about a half an hour to unload so I left the dog in the car with the windows down and unlocked the door for the driver. Fifteen minutes later I am standing in the kitchen when the driver comes in and says "Adam there is a cop out at your car."

"What the hell now?" I ask as I walk out back to see what is going on.

"Is this your car?" the cop asked with a tone of disgust.

"Yes it is." I replied.

"Is that your dog ?" was the stupidest question I had ever heard, but it was nonetheless the follow up by this true fighter of crime. He must have been a detective.

"No, actually that is my driver." is what I wanted to say (contrary to popular belief I am not that stupid.)

What I did say with just a slight hint of sarcasm was "Of course that is MY dog. That's why he is in MY car. Now what is the problem?"

"The problem is," he started "is that the people who work next door called and said that you leave the dog in your car out here every day from noon until four."

"That is total bullshit." I snapped back as I was truly pissed off at this point. "I normally don't even get here until four o'clock and the people next door are gone for the day by then."

"That's not what they said when they called this in." was his comeback.

"When they called it in? What is this, a fucking episode of Law And Order?" I was really losing it at this point.

"You might want to calm down a bit sir." he said with anger that I could feel was escalating along with my own. "If you are normally not here until four o'clock then why are you here now? And why is your dog with you?

"Do you see the delivery truck Columbo?" I knew I wasn't helping my cause but I just couldn't take it. "The driver called me and said he was going to be early so I came here to let him make his delivery."

"That doesn't answer my other question." He continued, "Why do you have the dog with you?"

"Not that is any of your business but there are real estate agents showing my condo right now." at this point I don't care if I get locked up. "Now, I'm guessing you don't own your own home. Not unless you call your mothers basement your own. But it's not a good idea to leave your dog home when potential buyers are walking through."

"I'm telling you right now sir," he began as his face turned four different shades of red. "if I come here again and see the dog in your car you will be arrested for cruelty to animals."

"Cruelty to animals?" I repeated in disbelief. "Take a good look at that dog. That fucking dog gets treated better than most people treat their first born and you are going to threaten me with cruelty to animals?"

"Consider yourself lucky today sir." he said as he walked back to his cruiser. "But if I see that dog again, I will arrest you."

"Tell your mommy I said hello." I muttered under my breath as he drove away.

About a half an hour later and after I had calmed down a bit I realized that I was lucky. I had let my temper get the better of me but didn't get locked up. All I can figure, is that maybe he did live in his mothers basement and I had embarrassed him to the point where he was reflecting on where he was at this stage of his life. I'm sure that's probably not the case but since I have no evidence to prove otherwise that is the story I am sticking with.

Quickie #9

Dumb Customer: "So let me get this straight. For $5 we get a movie, dinner, and drinks. Is that correct?"

Me: "Yes, we are actually a nonprofit organization founded with one clear purpose, to make your life as pleasurable as possible. If we take a loss, so be it. Now, if it is alright with you I am also going to spit shine your shoes."

Dumb Customer: "Is that free?"

Me: "Leave now before I get angry."

Chapter 11

Butch Lesbians

It's a relatively slow Sunday afternoon. About fifteen minutes after the movie starts, two women (bull dykes) and a male friend (obvious derelict) come in to see "The Notebook". Now, as anybody who has seen this movie knows it is not the type of flick that these three restraining orders waiting to happen would enjoy. So I gladly take their money and direct them into the correct theater. A half an hour later, just as I thought might happen, they come out to the lobby and ask for their money back because in their words "This fucking movie sucks."

"Well I am sorry to hear that." I started with (I am completely lying at this point but I know I'm going to enjoy these next few minutes. "We cannot refund your money for the tickets but if you would like to contact the company that produced the movie I'm sure they would be willing to reimburse you. You might just have to fill out a small questionnaire or survey for them."

The following exchange took place next.

Bull Dyke #1: "We want our money back now."

Me: "Not gonna happen."

Bull Dyke #2: "We want our money back now or there is going to be a problem."

Me:	"There already is a problem. I'm standing here listening to you neanderthals when I could be slitting my wrists."
Bull Dyke #2:	"This is fucking bullshit."
Me:	"Intelligent comeback."
Derelict:	"I'm going to wait outside because I'm on probation and can't get in anymore trouble." (My guess is that he had illegal sexual relations with a farm animal.)
Me:	"Wow. That is a shocker. I can't believe that a fine young man like that would ever have had trouble with the law."
Bull Dyke #1:	"Fuck you and give us our money back now."
Me:	"Would you like me to say this in trailer park speak so you will understand. NO FUCKING WAY WILL I GIVE YOU YOU'RE MONEY BACK. NOW LEAVE WITH THAT WANNA BE CRIMINAL FRIEND OF YOURS AND TIP OVER SOME UNSUSPECTING COWS, COOK UP SOME FUCKING ROADKILL, BRUSH YOUR ONE TOOTH, FUCK YOUR PET GOAT, SLEEP WITH YOUR COUSIN, CHEW SOME TOBACCI, DRINK SOME JACK, CUSTOMIZE YOUR 1974 FORD PICKUP WITH THE STICKER ON THE BACK THAT HAS CALVIN PISSING ON THE CHEVY LOGO, SAY YOUR DAILY PRAYERS TO THE LATE DALE EARNHARDT, AND TAKE YOUR MONTHLY HOSEDOWN. DO ANYTHING BUT TO CONTINUE STANDING HERE WASTING MY TIME. BECAUSE ALTHOUGH THE FIFTEEN BUCKS YOU WANT BACK MIGHT ACTUALLY BE ENOUGH TO PAY YOUR RENT FOR THE MONTH, NOT ALL OF US ARE AS WHITE TRASH PIECES OF SHIT LIKE YOU."
Bull Dyke #1:	"We'll never come back here again."

Me: "No shit. Problem solved."

   Surprisingly enough, I really have not seen them again. Which is kind of sad, because I've thought of so many more white trash clichés since then and I am just dying to use them. Sometimes I think half of my customers got lost on their way to a Larry the Cable Guy Show, and the other half are out of prison on a weekend furlough. Nonetheless, where would we be without them? In foodservice heaven, that's where.

Quickie #10

Dumb Customer: "$12 for a bottle of wine is expensive."

Me: "You don't get out much do you?"

Dumb Customer: "I can get this same bottle of wine at the liquor store for $9."

Me: "Well then, go pick up a bottle and I'll meet you there in a half an hour. Don't start the movie without me."

Chapter 12

Rubber Gun

The next story I am about to tell you, actually for a short period of time, had me second guessing the way I handled the situation. For a very short period of time that is.

It was a reasonably busy Sunday afternoon and one of the movies had just gone to credits. As always, I open the theater door and start helping the staff clean up. As I am cleaning one of the tables off I notice five empty mini wine bottles on the floor that were strategically placed to keep them out of sight until the movie was over.

Of course this is always going to send me into a tirade about cheap assholes always trying to beat the system. It will also lead me to my speech about how the waiters and waitresses have to keep an eye out for this kind of ignorance and alert me to it when it occurs. The reality is that this was not an always kind of time.

I instantly remembered the same thing had happened about a month before. Then it hit me like a Los Angeles patrolman's baton hitting Rodney King. The fat bastard that had walked out of the theater as I was walking in was the same moron from a month ago. Normally I would have noticed him and his Goodyear Blimp of a wife but it was just a really hectic night.

"Son of a bitch" I thought to myself. "I had the prick and let him slip right through my fingertips." Then, as though it was divine intervention, I happened to glance toward the lobby and I noticed that this fucking idiot was standing there waiting for Jabba the Hut (also known as the douchebag that married this shithead) to finish up in the bathroom.

In my mind I am thinking "This asshole is so arrogant that he does not care about the fact that what he just did is not only juvenile but also illegal. Then he has the balls to stick around afterwards while Shamu uses the bathroom.

What pissed me off the most was that if this asshole got away with this than it meant I was not doing my job. That is not something I can live with. This is all running through my head as I walk towards tons of (not so) fun and ask "You do realize that you can't bring in your own wine?"

"What are you talking about?" he muttered through the crumbs that were stuck in his unkempt goatee.

"You know exactly what I am talking about Omar the fucking tent maker. This is the second time that you and your Macys Day Parade float that you call a wife brought in your own wine. If you are too cheap to take Sasquatch out for a movie, dinner, and drinks than maybe you should stay home with five gallons of Ben and Jerry's, a box of the finest white zinfandel, and fond memories of the past when you could actually see your own prick and Tubby the Tuba actually wanted to see it."

My rant was over. But as I mentioned earlier there was a reason to second guess myself. My wife tells me on a daily basis that I need to think before I speak. This was one of those times where I should have listened. What this asshole did next was more surprising than when I found out that professional wrestling was staged.

"Do you know what this is?" He asked as he struggled to pull his wallet from his back pocket which was stretched to the brink by his enormous girth.

"A fucking badge" is all I could think to myself as he opened the wallet for probably the first time in twenty years.

The next two seconds seemed to take ten minutes as I thought of my options of how to answer this stunner of a question. If I back down than I am just giving in and inviting Butterbean and the Mrs. to do the same exact thing the next time they emerge from their winter hibernation. If I don't back down and this guy really works for an agency that can cause the cinema some serious problems than I am looking for another job the minute he makes the phone call that I am sure he would make. If I apologize . . . now wait, you and I both know that is not going to happen. I need to think fast and this is how I rationalized (or un-rationalized) what I was about to do next.

If he was really a cop would he be so blatant about it after I confronted him about an illegal act he had just committed? Is he just way too fat to be a cop? Does he work for the ABC? Is he flat out bluffing? Is he just way too fat to be a cop? (sorry did I say that already?)

"FUCK HIM AND THE HUNGRY HUNGRY HIPPO HE RODE IN ON" went through my head as I went on this most intelligent and thoroughly thought out response to the initial question he has posed to me. "Do you know what this is?"

"I know exactly what that is." I started "That is a badge and as a matter of fact I have one just like it. I got mine on sale at IPARTY one week after Halloween. Now I need to know is that where you got yours and did you pay full price? If that badge were real you would not flaunt it after being confronted about breaking the law. But just in case it is real could I get one more look at it? I want to make sure I get the badge number and the town that was dumb enough to hire you because I will be on the phone to that town police station by the time you get to your car."

Luckily for me he apparently was bluffing because the only person I have ever seen waddle out to their car faster than him was his wife.

The reason I second guessed myself was that my kneejerk reactions could have serious consequences on the cinema. I would never want that to happen but at the same time I am not going to bow down to some asshole that is just going to treat me and my staff as though we were doormats that they can just wipe their feet on. Not on my watch.

Quickie #11

Me: "Dina (dumb waitress), can you work New Years?"

Dumb Waitress: "What is the date?"

Me: "From now on, before you answer any questions, I need you to go into the bathroom, look into the mirror, say the answer into the mirror, and if the answer makes sense to you come back out and give your answer. Do you understand what I am saying?"

Dumb Waitress: "Not really, I still don't know what date you want me to work."

Me: "Forget it, I don't need you to do anything but tell my wife that the last words I spoke before I jumped head first in the fry-o-lator were I love you."

Chapter 13

Daughter's Birthday

It's a Friday night and some asshole decides to drop his sixteen year old daughter (immature bitch) and ten of her idiot friends off to see a movie. What he is basically saying to us is "Better you than me."

Of course it starts immediately. The kids won't shut up and they are very loud. At first I let it go because the movie has not started so they are not really bothering anyone yet. Then the movie starts, and the kids' behavior escalates. Every two minutes I have a waitress telling me that they are getting complaints from other customers about the kids.

I tell the waitress with the misfortune of having these morons in her section to ask them if they could please respect the other customers and keep the noise down. They basically laugh at her and see it as a reason to get even more obnoxious. She asks them a second time with the same result.

Now it is time for me to get involved. As is evidenced by the past, this is usually not a good thing for anybody. The end result does not often involve a happy ending for any of the involved parties. Why would this be any different? It wouldn't be.

I approach the table and very nicely inform them that if they can't act like adults and keep the noise down than they will be asked (told) to leave. Again, this just added fuel to the fire as they got even louder.

"Susan" I yell as she informs me of the latest complaint "Tell them to get the fuck out right now."

At this same time, I realize that these assholes ordered a shit load of food and it is coming to the window as I speak. If they leave I will have to throw it all away and that's a lot of money lost.

"Box it up quickly." I say to the guys in the kitchen. "They need to wait for the bitch's father to pick them up. That asshole is paying for this."

I walk back into the lobby where the young assholes have all congregated. The birthday bitch is on her cell phone explaining her version of the events to daddy dickhead. I'll tell you one thing, her recollections differed quite a bit from mine. She should probably try some ginkgo biloba because a young girl like that shouldn't have problems remembering what had happened just five minutes ago.

Approximately ten minutes later, the father showed up and he was not happy. The big problem here was that he was upset with me and not the fact that his little princess and her merry band of shitheads didn't know how to behave in public. At this point I don't care if he is pissed off. I've been pissed since he dropped the village idiots off on me in the first place. So join the club fuck nuts because this one is on you.

"Are you trying to ruin Angela's birthday?" he screamed.

"Who is Angela?" I answer sarcastically.

"My daughter." he replied while pointing to the bitch.

"Ohhhh, that's Angela." I say with the sincerity of serial killer at a parole hearing. "Well then, yes, I am trying to ruin her birthday. Quite honestly, this morning it wasn't high on my to do list but about an hour ago it jumped right to the top. It even knocked getting a root canal out of the top ten. At this point I'm rethinking that decision though. I really think the root canal would have been less painful. By the way, here is your bill."

"You expect me to pay that bill?" he asked in disbelief.

"Well, let's see." I started. "They ordered all the food. We cooked all the food. All the food is right here for you to take with you. So, yes I expect you to pay this bill. The tip is up to your discretion."

"The only way that I am going to pay the bill is if you give these kids free movie passes." He stated quite surprisingly to me.

"That's not going to happen." I snapped back. "Why the fuck would I give them incentive to come back here? They disturbed every other customer in the theater. I don't want these morons back here as paying customers, never mind using free passes."

"It is the only way that bill gets paid." he said matter of fact.

At this point I decided to bluff. A bluff that I would unfortunately, be called on.

"If you don't pay the bill then I will be forced to call the police and report a theft." I said with no intentions of ever having to make that call.

"Go ahead." He responded. "I'll wait."

You have got to be fucking kidding me. The whole reason we are in this situation in the first place is that this guy's daughter and her friends were acting like assholes. Now this dickhead is going to be so stubborn that he is willing to let the cops get involved. I should probably stop playing poker because apparently I suck at bluffing.

I go to the kitchen to get the phone still hoping that he will cave before I have to do this. As I start dialing I realize that I am going to have to go through with this because this asshole just won't back down. I explain the situation to the dispatcher and she informs me an officer will be here shortly. What she didn't tell me was that the officer coming would be about as useful to me as sleeves on a vest.

Sheriff Rosco P. Coltrane shows up a few minutes later and I quickly realize that I am basically on my own. I bring him up to speed on the situation and he shows about as much interest in helping me as Dr. Sheldon Cooper has interest in coitus. Absolutely none.

"Why don't you just give him some free passes?" He says to me. "Then he will pay his bill and go. We can all get on with our night."

"The only thing I want to give him is a punch in the face. He owes me for that food and I want the money." I snapped.

"He's not budging," Rosco continued, "so please give him some passes so I can get back to what I was in the middle of."

"Your secluded parking spot at the abandoned factory where you take your four hour naps will still be there when you get back. This asshole owes me $150. Your job is to serve and protect. Now serve your purpose and protect me from basically getting robbed you gutless wannabe crime fighter." is exactly what I wanted to say.

You would be crazier than Gary Busey if you think I actually said that. I'm no Albert Einstein but I'm no Jersey Shore cast member either. I took a few seconds to calm myself down and realized it was best for business to end this and get the cop and the assholes out of the lobby. So I reluctantly gave them free passes and the dickhead reluctantly paid his bill.

This one pisses me off more than most other incidents because the people in the wrong are the ones that came out on top. They had no interest in watching a movie that night so getting thrown out had no affect on them. They all got a free pass to come back. The cop got paid for not doing his job. Myself and the rest of the staff lost because we have to deal with theses assholes when they come back. But I will remember them if they do decide to come back.

As Rosco was walking out I just couldn't help myself. "Excuse me officer" I began "Are there any other establishments in town I can get free stuff for acting like an asshole?"

"What was that?" he responded "I don't think I understood you."

"Not surprising." I said with a big shit eating grin. "Forget about it. Have a WONDERFUL night."

Quickie #12

Dumb Customer upon returning from the bathroom: "I can't remember which theater I was in."

Me: "What movie were you watching?"

Dumb Customer: "Sixth Sense."

Me: "I'm going to go out on a limb here and say that it's probably the one that says "Sixth Sense" above the door."

Dumb Customer: "Good point. Thanks."

Me: "WOW."

Chapter 14

Do I Have a What?

This story is actually quite embarrassing to me. It is however quite humorous to my wife. The reason it is embarrassing to me is that it is one of the few times I have been left speechless and humiliated by my actions. The reason it is humorous to my wife is that I called her in a panic looking for advice then basically threw that advice out the window and hid like a dog that had just been caught chewing on Charlie Sheens favorite porno.

It's about nine thirty on a Tuesday night. I have sent everybody home because there are only about ten customers. I look out into the lobby and see a fourteen or fifteen year old female customer that appears to be looking for something.

"Can I help you with something?" I ask as I walk out of the kitchen.

"Where is the waitress?" she asks.

"I sent her home because it is so slow." I answer. "Is there something I can get for you?"

What she asked me next will forever be burned into my memory. It is a question that not only did I never expect to have to answer in my lifetime, I definitely never expected to have to answer it to a teenage stranger.

"Do you have a tampon?" she asked with the same ease of someone asking me if I could pass the salt.

Talk about being blindsided. I was shocked and dumbfounded and panicked and almost wet myself. All I could do and say was absolutely nothing. I just stood there with a blank look on my face for about thirty seconds. When I could actually move my extremities I ran to the kitchen faster than Usain Bolt.

Once in the kitchen, I called my wife with the urgency of a 911 caller reporting a murder (though I was probably more shaken up).

"You won't believe what this teenage girl just asked me." I said hyperventilating. "She asked me if I had a tampon. What the fuck do I do?"

For approximately the next two to three minutes all I heard on the other end of the line was gut-busting laughter. When my very sympathetic wife composed herself long enough to speak, she gave me this advice. Actually, I'm not going to tell you what she said I should do. Those words will never be spoken by me to anyone especially to a teenage girl.

For the guys out there you probably have no clue as to what that advice might have been and I hope you never will. For the women you probably do. You can explain it to the guys if you want, but I assure you that they really don't want to know.

I spent the rest of the night hiding in the kitchen. When the movie ended I dropped the checks on the tables and ran back to the kitchen hoping that no one needed any change. I went back out five minutes later and everybody was gone. Thank you God.

The only funny thing that I take out of that night is of all the problems and confrontations I have had with customers over the years the only one to ever shut me up completely was this teenage girl who just asked for help.

My wife on the other hand still thinks the whole ordeal is the funniest thing in the history of the world. She loves to tell the story every chance she gets. I don't try to stop her anymore because she put up with enough of my stories over the years. I'll let her have this one.

Quickie #13

Dumb Customer: "Why didn't you tell me this movie sucked so bad?"

Me: "You didn't ask."

Dumb Customer: "Well, you should have told me anyway."

Me: "OK then, if we are being honest I will tell you what I think. You're fat, your wife is ugly, your mullet is ridiculous, and your breath is really bad. Anything else that you want my opinion on? Wait, where are you going ? I'm ready to share."

Chapter 15

What the Fuck Happened to You?

This is a question that I sincerely hope you never have to answer. If you have had to answer it just one time, I can without the shadow of a doubt prove you have had to answer it a hundred times.

My personal misery with this question started on a busy Friday night. Everything seemed to be running smoothly. I'm scanning the lobby to get a feel of how the night might play itself out (believe it or not, after so many nights dealing with the public you get a sense early on how the rest of the night will turn out). Unfortunately, on this night my expectations for the evening turned out to be very premature and misguided.

Out of the corner of my eye I noticed three young men (poster children for birth control) giving the girl selling tickets a hard time. By the time I got to the booth to ask the girl what the problem was the guys were in the theater.

"What just happened?" I asked.

"They were just pissed that I made them show me an I.D. to see an R-rated movie" she answered.

"I assume they all showed proof that they were old enough." I asked.

"Yes" she answered. "As a matter of fact one of them was actually twenty one."

"Oh shit" I said. "Are you telling me that only one out of the three is old enough to drink?"

"Yes" she whispered. "His birthday was just last week."

This is terrible news to me. This is a recipe for disaster. It's an equation that only has horrible results. Will Hunting on his best day would have a hard time explaining this one.

X = asshole

XY = older asshole

2X + XY = 3 fucking assholes

I know it's confusing, but you'll just have to trust me on this one. I know from past experience that there are two potential scenarios with these shitheads. I also know that neither scenario works out well for any of us.

The first scenario involves the oldest shithead ordering a beer and rubbing it in his friends face that he is the only one who can partake in such libations. He did that very well.

The other scenario was him ordering beers and then trying to give them to his friends. Surprisingly enough he never tried the second scenario. I know this because I watched him like Mia Farrow watches Woody Allen when he's "got" the kids.

Everything was fine until the movie ended. I'm still not convinced that these three are model citizens. I watch them all the way from their seats. The "OLD" one is walking out with his beer.

"No he is not." I say to myself (I tend to talk to myself a lot).

The only problem with what I did next is that I didn't tell anybody I work with what I was about to do. My bad. Oh well, it happens.

I caught up with the moron and informed him that he was not permitted to take his drink outside with him. The big words must have confused him because he hesitated for a minute. As far as I can understand from my limited knowledge of the Neanderthal language his eventual response was "Why not?"

"Because, its fucking illegal. You fucking half breed." (I said that out loud didn't I?)

Yes, I did say that out loud and for reasons I still can't fathom, I think he took offense. His friends seemed pretty worked up also. I had disrespected their almighty. The one dickhead who was a big enough asshole for all of them. They were going to teach me a lesson.

Their problem was that I develop a learning disability when the teachers are douchebags. So when he decided to try and finish his drink outside I decided to pull it out of his hand, subsequently dumping it all over his face and shirt.

This is when me not telling anybody that I was going outside comes into play. It is now me and three pissed off assholes. It was as if Michael Buffer himself was there and I heard him bellow "Let's Get Ready To Rumble." Then I heard the ding ding of the opening bell. Before I knew it there was one asshole on my left arm and an even bigger asshole on my right. Then I looked up to see a fist with a big class ring on one of the fingers coming down to blast my left cheek. As much as I realized I was about to feel serious pain all that kept going through my mind was when the hell did they start giving out class rings for finishing the third grade?

That fucking unwarranted class ring had just split me wide open. I have three older brothers and have taken many beatings over the years. It was going to take a lot more than that to stop me. All it really did was piss me off even more.

"You're a fucking pussy!" I screamed. (Yes, that was the best I could come up with.)

"You're calling me a pussy?" he asked. "Why are you the one bleeding?"

"Because these two simpletons (Yes, someone that uses the fuck word as much as I do is calling somebody else simpletons) are holding my arms so I can't defend myself. Tell these poster children for birth control to let me go and we'll see who ends up the bloodiest you fucking puke. I'm going to rip your fucking head off and shove it up your ass so you can hear me kicking your butt. And the fucking moron twins will be next." The words were just spewing out of my mouth and I couldn't control it. I was feeling a rage that I had never felt before or since. "I am going to enjoy beating the shit out of you three jerkoffs like I have never enjoyed anything in life before."

"Let's get out of here." was the next thing I heard as they ran towards the parking lot. I started running after them but for reasons I still can't understand I made the smart decision for one of the few times in my life. I stopped. If I had caught up with them it still would have been three on one. Although I have had dreams of being in a three on one before, the three in those dreams are females.

I just stood there for a minute thinking that if it were ten years earlier I probably would have gone after them and who knows what the result would have been. Maybe I was growing up after all. Now it was time to go inside and check the damages.

"What the hell happened to you?" was the question asked of me by the first staff member to see me.

"Nothing" I uttered in disgust as I walked to the bathroom.

"Should I call the cops ?" was the follow up.

"Don't bother." I snapped back. "The assholes are long gone."

I took a look into the bathroom mirror and there it was. A two inch gash just below my left eye. Although it wasn't showing yet I knew my eye would also be black and blue very shortly. So that was the start of it. For the next month, I found myself answering the same question over and over.

WHAT THE FUCK HAPPENED TO YOU?

All Done

I, unfortunately, have many more of these ridiculous stories that I could share with you but I just need to stop.

My customers turned me into a very jaded person. I let it bother me so much more than I should have. Even though I gave it back to them, I still had it in the back of my mind for days. I can remember an incident with a disgruntled (fucking ignorant) customer that I had 10 years ago like it was yesterday. I realized it was time to let it go. This is my attempt to do that.

As long as I wake up every morning with my wife next to me and the dog waiting to be taken out than I am happy. What happened yesterday does not matter (unless the fucking Giants beat the Patriots in the Super Bowl AGAIN).

Anyone who has worked in the industry should please take my advice. Don't take it home with you. Don't let it linger. Realize that an asshole is going to be an asshole no matter how well you treat them. You can't change these people. Most of all if it works for you just write about it. It worked for me and I would love to hear other stories. We need to stick together.

Thank You, Thank You, Thank You, FUCK YOU, Thank You, Thank You, and Don't Let Me Forget Thank You

There are many people I need to say thanks to for this book. One person stands alone at the top of that list. I could not have done this without the patience and guidance of my tolerant, patient, smart, patient, beautiful, patient, understanding, patient, funny, patient, flexible, patient, wife Shelley. I have done the research and in most languages Shelley translates into "hot chick with a short memory and a huge heart."

In all seriousness, Shelley is the reason I get out of bed every morning. She put up with me through good times and bad. She never wavered in her love for me. She listened to me rant about assholes more times than I care to remember. I just want her to know how much I love her because I don't think I tell her enough. Thank you, I love you!

Thank You Jason Miranda.

Jason started out as a coworker. He was 10 years younger than me and I started out thinking that a work relationship was all it would ever be. Fortunately I was wrong, (motherfucker, that's about six times now). Jason became one of my best friends. If it wasn't for Jason I would probably be doing thirty-five to life for employee on patron homicide. He had my back on more than one occasion and I thank him for that.

Thank You Chris

My brother Chris is the owner of the Cinema Pub. He gave me the latitude to deal with the shithead customers in a way I deemed warranted.

He also did a lot more to better my life than I could explain in these pages without breaking down. So, all I want to say is thank you Chris.

Fuck You Assholes

I really want to say thank you (fuck you) to all the assholes who made me start writing all this shit down in the first place. The customers. I know I am repeating myself, but if it were not for you, I would have nothing to bitch about. You made me realize that there are a lot more idiots in this world than I had originally thought. (All I had on my list were Michael Moore, Bill Maher, and Snooki). Seriously though, if not for your ignorance I would have nothing to bitch about.

Thank You Mom and Dad

I want to say thank you to my parents. My parents raised eight children the right way. They taught us that hard work was the way to live your life. Nothing was ever going to be given to you. They taught us to treat people the same way that we would want to be treated. That is probably why I had such a short temper when it came to disrespectful customers and I am proud of that. I thank you both so very much. I love you.

Thank You Janine, Chris, Mark, Greg, Jen, Justine, Jeremy, my brothers and sisters.

They listened to me babble on about this shit for years. Never once did any of them tell me to shut up and deal with it. They encouraged me at all times and kept me on track when I was veering way off the track. To all of you I want to say I love you.

A Redundant Thank You

I am probably one of the most difficult people on the planet to live with. I have a bad temper. I don't deal with ignorance very well. I bottle things up and then let them explode. At the risk of sounding like a broken record I have to thank Shelley one more time. No one other than her I can think of would have put up with some of the rants I have gone on. Shelley, thank you.

About the Author

This is Adam Ballarino's first book. It is based on the ten years he worked in the food service industry. The ten years he refers to as "The most miserable of my life."

Adam lives with his wife Shelley and their dog Fast Eddie in the same small town he grew up in. He is currently a supervisor for a third party logistics company.

Printed in Great Britain
by Amazon